The Fabian Society

The Fabian Society has played a central role for more than a century in the development of political ideas and public policy on the left of centre. Analysing the key challenges facing the UK and the rest of the industrialised world in a changing society and global economy, the Society's programme aims to explore the political ideas and the policy reforms which will define progressive politics in the new century.

The Society is unique among think tanks in being a democratically-constituted membership organisation. It is affiliated to the Labour Party but is editorially and organisationally independent. Through its publications, seminars and conferences, the Society provides an arena for open-minded public debate.

D0542339

Fabian Society
11 Dartmouth Street
London SW1H 9BN
www.fabian-society.org.uk

 Fabian ideas
Series editor: Ellie Levenson

First published June 2003

ISBN 0 7163 0607 7
ISSN 1469 0136

British Library Cataloguing in Publication data.
A catalogue record for this book is available from the British Library.

Printed by Bell & Bain Limited, Glasgow

This pamphlet is kindly supported by

the Co-operative Group

Contents

About the author

Hazel Blears has been Member of Parliament for Salford since 1997 and is Minister for Public Health.

Acknowledgements

I would like to place on record my thanks to the following: to Paul Richards for his original idea of the pamphlet, and for excellent research and advice throughout; to Bernard Crick for his inspiration; to all those who kindly gave their time, advice and criticism at a Fabian seminar and as readers of the first drafts; to Ellie Levenson at the Fabian Society for her patience; to the Co-operative Group for their support and encouragement; to Chris Dabbs and Lance Gardner for their commitment to risk taking and ideas that can work; and most of all to the people in the communities who are already in control and showing us the way.

The Fabian Society would also like to thank the Co-operative Group for their generous support in funding this pamphlet. As always, it is recognised that their support for the project does not imply that this report reflects their views.

Introduction

'A socialist society that is true to its egalitarian principles of human brotherhood must rest on the widest possible diffusion of power and responsibility, so as to enlist the active participation of as many as possible of its citizens in the tasks of democratic self-government.'
GDH Cole

Governments need to be able to tell a story about where they are going and what they want to achieve. For Labour the narrative has to be more ambitious than just spending more money on public services than the Tories. We need to show that we trust local people to direct, own and manage their local public services.

To achieve this we need to rethink and update 'community' as a socialist value, and let the new realities of community be reflected in our policies.

In particular this means recasting the idea of 'public ownership' to mean real, not theoretical or imagined, ownership, over public services by local people. Decentralisation and mutualisation should be the guiding principles of public service reform. Key parts of the public services should be made into mutual organisations owned and controlled by local people and by their users.

1

In order to pass power to the people, we need to create an active citizenry, capable of taking responsibility. This means creating a new cadre of community leaders and social entrepreneurs, unlocking 'the extraordinary potential of ordinary people'.

A new citizens' participation agency (CPA) should be created to engage a new layer of activists. This new agency should be local, flexible, and innovative and help to create a new culture of public service and active citizenship. There should be new incentives both practical and financial to encourage and support active citizens.

Without creating a tangible connection between citizens and their public services, beyond narrow concepts of consultation and participation, the process of alienation and disengagement from mainstream politics and institutions will continue. But if we succeed in creating decentralised community ownership over public services, the prize will be a renaissance of civil society, mutuality, and political life – the historic goals of radicals, reformers and socialists.

“

1| Labour's story

It is a commonplace that political parties need 'narratives' or 'stories' to explain to voters what they stand for and the direction in which they seek to take society. As we enter the midpoint of the second term and begin to think about the next election, we need to ask: what is Labour's story now?

In the period 1994-2001, much of Labour's programme was defined by a rejection of its own recent history. The prefix 'new' was constructed by the party's campaigners to distinguish it from the 'old' Labour Party. The party under Tony Blair went through a conscious period of patiently explaining what Labour was not. Our approach to the electorate was as much about reassurance as radicalism.

This changed in 2001. Labour's landslide victory in the general election came after a campaign based on a clear choice between public investment and public spending cuts. The campaign revealed the deep fault-lines in British politics, and gave us a clear indication that most people supported Labour's ambitions for the public services. But the question now is whether simply being the party of public services is enough of a governing narrative for Labour.

My argument in this pamphlet is that Labour must prove that we are more than merely the party of the public services and the public sector, and that our radical credentials run much deeper than simply wanting to restore two decades of Tory under-investment in schools, hospitals, roads, public buildings, parks and social services. Winding back the clock to 1979, as though that era was some socialist utopia, is hardly an ambition worthy of our party.

The radical position in politics today, and the narrative that Labour needs to articulate, is about a new vision of the public realm, where public services are a pillar in a changed and strengthened society, where the relationships between customers and suppliers, governors and governed, individuals and society, and individuals and each other are transformed. More investment in public services takes us some of the way on the journey, and must be delivered and protected from those who want to cut back. But our destination is far more exciting and ambitious. So what is this new vision of the public realm? It is about:

- Empowering people to take decisions about the priorities and direction of local public services
- Giving people ownership and a stake in the running of public services
- Devolving power and opportunity within the public services to local communities.

In short, it is about taking power away from the politicians, the 'experts', the bureaucrats and the officials, and passing it to the people. This is a bold ambition, because those with power are almost always reluctant to give it up.

As David Marquand pointed out in an essay before the 1997 election, a new community politics must be 'bottom-up, not top-down. It will shy away from universal solutions and all embracing formulae; it will run with the grain of human igno-rance... it will be an extraordinary difficult and demanding politics, requiring levels of humility and openness from which the political class of today falls abysmally short.'

This new approach goes far beyond current concepts of 'community consultation'. The attempts by councils and others to engage people through citizens' panels, juries and forums and wider consultation exercises are desirable and stand as the best ways of helping service providers understand and anticipate their clients' needs. But consultation is not the same as real participation and ownership. The consultation model means that the power still rests with the service providers, not the client community. In working-class areas, it is still the professionals who are in charge, regardless of how much consultation is conducted. The consultation model helps local people become more engaged in local political processes, but does not alter the underlying power structures. Being asked what you think is fine, but real ownership comes from being involved in the planning, financing, organisation, delivery and evaluation of a public service.

'Power to the people' is an old slogan, but might also be an idea whose time has come. Empowering local communities to take control through genuine citizenship and genuine ownership, and thus engendering a new set of relationships between the people and their government, should be at the heart of Labour's governing narrative. It makes a reality of John Smith's wonderful ambition for Labour to release 'the extra-ordinary potential of ordinary people.'

This pamphlet is written to make the case for greater local, community control over public services, for greater mutual and co-operative ownership over assets and activities, and for a new spirit of active citizenship, backed by a new national body, the Citizens' Participation Agency. It does not pretend to provide a detailed blueprint for new structures; it makes a political rather than a technical argument. It is an argument which I believe will gain greater support as our reforms of public services and political institutions gather pace.

2| Understanding community

I f we seek to empower local communities, we must be clear what we mean. This is a discussion filled with potential misunderstandings.

As a political term, community – like freedom, equality and democracy – tends to mean what politicians want it to mean. 'The community' is invoked like a muse, to provide political cover, to imply democratic legitimacy, and to sweeten the pill. Who could argue with the building of 'community centres' or employing 'community nurses'? We have community colleges, community funds, the new deal for communities, community chests, and so on.

For socialists, the lack of a clear meaning for the term community is more than semantic. The confusion creates a barrier to devising policies which are in line with our values. We have to be clear what is meant by the words we use, and although political terms are always contested, we need as broad a consensus as possible around the things we stand for.

It is notable that of all the democratic socialist values – liberty, equality and fraternity – it is the last, what we would generally describe today as community, which has remained the most elusive. (The Italian political theorist Noberto Bobbio describes it as 'indeterminate.') Bernard Crick points out that of socialism's three defining principles community is 'the most rhetorical, potent, but least defined of values.'

For some socialists community has been simply a synonym for 'the people' or 'society' or even 'the state', and an antonym to 'the private sector' and 'competition'.

For others, 'community' signified the long-gone certainties of working class and trade union solidarity. But this stereotypical image of traditional working class communities was never accurate. The building where I have my constituency office in Salford is also home to the Working Class Movement Library. Its vast collection of letters, posters, leaflets, pamphlets and books attests to the extraordinary richness and variety of working class experience since the industrial revolution. Through its trade unions, craft associations, corresponding societies, friendly societies, co-operatives, women's organisations, religious organisations, sports and social clubs, campaigns and causes and a million other voluntary organisations the working class in Salford, as elsewhere, was a highly stratified, varied and complex organism. Meanwhile the 'community' portrayed in Salford's other great cultural contribution, Coronation Street, where back doors are left unlocked, neighbours know one another, and life coalesces around the local pub and corner shop, is a world which belongs today almost entirely in fiction.

Sociologists such as Robert Puttnam and Richard Sennett have documented the breakdown of traditional social ties and mutuality in advanced democratic societies. This is characterised by falling membership of social, political and religious organisations and falling levels of voter registration and turnouts. The traditional norms of social cohesion, and the social glue provided by the organisations of civil society, have been eroded, perhaps forever. So any definition of community based on them is doomed to be outdated.

A more useful notion of community is as a way of expressing

fellowship, or a sense of belonging to one another in a society. In a world of insecurity and globalisation, of a decline of trust and deference, this can be seen as more helpful and attractive. It is used as shorthand for the concept of the interdependence and mutuality of individuals and collections of people. A belief in the importance of mutuality and reciprocity differentiates socialism from liberalism or conservatism, and is the antidote to the idea that we are all atomised individuals in economic competition with one another. This use of community is the one which appears as a theme in the new Clause IV of the Labour Party's constitution, where: 'by the strength of our common endeavour we achieve more than we achieve alone, ... and where we live together, freely, in a spirit of solidarity, tolerance and respect.'

This definition came about as part of Labour's conscious and deliberate political reconstruction in the mid-nineties. Some have indeed seen it as a defining characteristic of New Labour. Joel Krieger, for example, argues that: 'There is no mistaking the importance of community for New Labour. In fact, it seems clear that, in narratives of community, it finds its moral voice and locates a comfortable third way ethos to guide institutional and policy innovation.'

New Labour's use of community as interdependence borrows from much older ethical strands of socialism and radicalism. William Morris said that 'fellowship is life; lack of fellowship is death'. And it was the early Christian socialists who sought to apply the biblical command that 'we are our brother's keeper' to contemporary society's ills.

Yet even this concept fails to define fully what we mean by community. A vague sense of being nice to one another, whilst laudable, is not a sustainable governing narrative. It leaves too many questions and loose ends. Who are the community? Those who can shout the loudest? Those who make the most articulate and convincing campaigners? Those who have been in a location the longest? Those who claim to represent local people through the ballot box? The leaders of ethnic or faith groups? Is the community all of us – or any of us? Can you belong to more than one community, and if so, which has primacy? How do we balance the rights of competing communities?

Community may mean fellowship, belonging, group identity, and security for its members. But that need not be a positive thing. These feelings can be fostered by street gangs, football hooligans, criminal fraternities, or fascist parties – communities which run entirely counter to the public good. The role and rights of communities might run into direct conflict with the rights of other communities, or of individuals.

So however interdependent they may be, communities cannot ever be entirely self-policing and self-run, contrary to the views of hard-line communitarians such as Amiti Etzioni, whose writings enjoyed something of a vogue in the mid-nineties. There will always be the need for mediation between communities and for a higher authority of rules and laws, no matter how devolved our systems of decision-making and governance.

So if community does not mean 'fraternity' as class solidarity (real or imagined), or simply interdependence and kinship, then what does it mean for the left today?

Democratic community

We need to develop an understanding of community which does two things. It must withstand theoretical testing and debate; and it must be applicable to public policy.

Community must mean more than simply a common bond between individuals, or a sense of belonging and obligation. A socialist definition must include a dimension of empowerment and control over people's collective destiny. As Bernard Crick argued in his book *Socialism*: 'A fraternal society would be one in which there would be far more popular participation in deciding how decisions are to be made.'

Our utilisation of the term community must mean therefore a democratic community in which members of the community have a real say over the decisions affecting them, active participation in systems of decision-making and governance, ownership over local assets, and the ability to hold to account their representatives.

This gets us closer to a modern understanding of the characteristics and value of community:

- There is no such thing as 'the community' as a homogeneous entity. There are many and over-lapping communities, with new forms developing all the time. Some are chosen by their members, some are the product of ascribed characteristics
- Communities exist beyond geography; they encompass a wide range of social ties and common interests which go beyond proximity or common residence
- Communities benefit and enhance the lives of individuals, through fellowship, development and learning, and engendering a strong sense of mutual rights and responsibilities
- Communities can give the individual a sense of identity and culture
- Communities must be democratic, giving people a collective say over their destinies
- Communities must be tolerant towards, and respect other communities, and where disputes arise, there must be mediation by law
- Communities, in their diverse forms, create a civic society where the forces of decency can act countervail anti-social behaviour

Community is usually expressed through association with

others in voluntary institutions. The decline in traditional forms of association has led some to argue that civic society is breaking down. Organisations based around common cultural, faith, political or recreational activities have witnessed a real decline in recent years. It is demonstrably true to say that many traditional organisations, mostly founded in the Victorian era, are facing real difficulties in recruiting, retaining and energising their members. This is as true of the major political parties, including Labour, as it is of the Salvation Army, the Boys' Clubs, the Girl Guides, and the Church of England.

But other writers, for example Paul Richards in his Fabian pamphlet *Is the Party Over?*, have shown that many organisations have found ways to re-define activism, involve members and re-invent their roles. As the case studies later in this pamphlet show, many new organisations, by redefining activism and giving people a real say, have managed to reverse the trend towards disengagement. This mosaic of new voluntary associations and organisations is part of the modern community, replacing the old certainties of local church, union, club and charity, but providing the glue which can hold communities together.

The British are still joiners of organisations – it is the forms of organisation that are changing, not the underlying desire to take part. Even in the most deprived neighbourhoods in Britain there is still an extant civil society and a stock of 'social capital' which can be mobilised and built on.

Community is expressed through association as well as through geography. Traditional forms of community were based on a neighbourhood or town, factory or trade, religion or ethic background. These forms were largely determined forms of community, and could be intolerant and restrictive. Modern communities are more often elective forms of community, with members choosing to join.

The rise of the internet allows forms of interaction, shared rules

and assumptions, and bonds between individuals which tran-
scend nations, religions and continents. We are only at the beginning of this development, and through the democratisation of
information and technology, new global communities are
increasingly being created.

These are increasingly communities based on common interests and lifestyles, not on locality. Older people, young people,
people from different faith groups or ethnic backgrounds, or
people with different hobbies or interests may feel a stronger
sense of kinship with their like-minded fellows, regardless of
where they live, than their immediate neighbours. Recognising
the importance of this form of community should inform our
overall approach.

"

3 | Real public ownership

Why does any of this theory matter? I believe that in order to transform our society, and dramatically to improve the life chances of the people Labour represents, we need to move further and faster in a socialist direction. We need to recast the traditional structures and institutions of the state, including 'our' institutions such as the National Health Service, educational institutions, and social services.

An understanding of the nature of community informs the next stage of my argument: that we need genuine community empowerment and community ownership over the delivery of public services. The old Fabian model – of an enlightened class of administrators and bureaucrats running services on behalf of the people – no longer works, if it ever did. The leitmotif of Labour's approach to the public realm is that public services do not need more altruistic public servants, they need ownership by the public.

Real versus imagined ownership

Here I mean real, actual, legal ownership by local people of key services. This must be within a national framework of standards and regulation, and within the boundaries of a broader public good. But it is genuine ownership – beyond consultation, representation on management boards, and 'participation' in decision-making. It means shifting real power, opportunity – and responsibility – into the hands of working people.

On the left we have created an imagined ownership based on what the state owns. Public buildings such as libraries, museums and town halls, public institutions such as schools, colleges and parks, and public services from health to social services belong to all of us (in theory) because traditionally they are owned, managed and run by the state. But there is a huge gap between theoretical ownership of a state institution, and real ownership of a community institution. The first rests on a woolly sense of 'public ownership' irrespective of whether local people have any say or feel any stake. The latter means local people own, manage, direct and control a local institution.

There is of course a theoretical barrier here: if ownership is taken from the whole public, and passed to an active section of the public, are those not actively involved in running a local service deprived of an aspect of their citizenship?

I would argue that the basis of 'public ownership' over public services is so shaky in practice that a shift from imagined to real ownership would be welcomed by local people and be a marked improvement on the current situation. For millions of low-income people in Britain, who are the most reliant on public services, the best we have managed so far are 'poor services for poor people' in Richard Titmuss' devastating phrase.

Mutuality and public ownership

Labour's adherence to the state model of public ownership has arisen in part because of a false dichotomy in political debate between the free market and the centralised state. Either you were a Thatcherite, or you were a Bennite. Seeing ownership in this black and white way ignores ignores the rich tradition of co-operative and mutual enterprise which can give us inspiration in tackling today's problems.

Nationalisation of the kind exercised by the Labour Government of 1945 may have been the best solution to the social and economic problems of the time. State ownership of major sections of industry in peacetime was a natural progression of their control by the state in wartime. It belonged in a world of monolithic national institutions and bodies, of rationing and controls, and of a population in military uniform.

But it was seen by many socialists, even at the time, as a means to an end, not as the end in itself. For example GDH Cole wrote in 1943 that: 'I can imagine no society which ought not to do its best to give to all its members an equal chance, an assured basic standard of living, and as much democratic freedom as possible. These things are ends, which all decent men ought at all times to desire and attempt to further. The communal ownership of the means of production is a method of bringing them about, appropriate in the main to the type of society in which you and I are living, but not in any sense morally imperative in all societies, irrespective of time and place.'

Since the 1940s, thanks to revisionists from Crosland to Kinnock and Blair, we have constructed a democratic socialism which does not depend for its definition on a single model of state ownership.

A modern view of public ownership is anchored in different, non-state forms of social ownership, such as mutuality, employee participation, co-operative enterprise, and the rise of the social entrepreneur. It does not rest on the idea that the man in Whitehall knows best, or that public ownership means the same as state ownership.

This new concept of community ownership borrows heavily from traditional influences like the co-operative movement, but for it to work it must take account of modern conditions, challenges and constraints. Many Labour people have been happy to argue that the co-operative and mutual model is useful for parts of the commercial sector, such as retail, or 'added-value' parts of the public services and small community organisations. I want the mutual idea to apply to essential, statutory areas of public services, hitherto run by the central state.

A mutual is an enterprise owned by its members, which provides a variety of services to its members for their benefit. Mutuality may be used to describe mutual models of ownership or decision-making, mutual methods of doing business or simply a mutual ethos. Examples of mutuals include agricultural co-operatives, building societies, banking mutuals and credit unions, communications co-operatives and co-operative internet service providers, energy co-operatives, fishing co-operatives, health provision and insurance mutuals, housing co-operatives, mutual insurers, tourism and worker co-operatives. There are over 700 million members of such organisations worldwide.

In the UK over recent years there has been a huge upsurge in mutual organisations: credit unions, social firms, housing co-operatives, fair-trade companies, farmers' markets, time banks, community banks, tenant-owned housing schemes, football supporters' trusts, and other forms of community ownership. What these projects and organisations have in common is their mutuality, which means they involve communities of people in common concerns for the common good. The profit motive becomes subservient to broader social aims.

New models of governance

In practical terms, putting communities in control of public services therefore means creating new forms of mutual governance for public services. There has been a great deal of work done on models and structures by various think tanks over recent years. Our thinking on this needs to be imaginative and rigorous.

Legally, amongst a range of options are new forms of public

interest company, defined in law, which provide for public interest goals and different kinds of 'stakeholder'-based governing boards, as recently endorsed by the Prime Minister's Strategy Unit. The Institute for Public Policy Research (IPPR) has published a helpful guide to existing public interest companies, from Network Rail and National Air Traffic Services to urban regeneration companies and further education colleges. The Office of Public Management (OPM) has also produced work on public interest companies, drawing on the US experience of public benefit corporations. An alternative model is a strengthened form of industrial and provident society (IPS), a co-operative for the benefit either of individual shareholding members or the wider stakeholding community.

We should also investigate and promote the idea of community ownership through new types of share schemes and co-operative ventures. This might include for example individual shares – and actual equity – in a GPs' surgery or health centre being owned by members of the local community. It is this co-operative principle which will be applied to NHS foundation trusts, with membership open to the local community, users, staff and other stakeholders. This gives real local ownership and governance.

One possiblity is that every adult voter in the geographical area served by a hospital or primary care trust, school, college, social service – or even parks and leisure facilities – should be given a vote to elect some or all of the non-executive directors as part of a stakeholder board. There might be a form of electoral college with votes distributed amongst staff, patients, voluntary groups, and residents. Some of the members of governing bodies might be chosen randomly for a prescribed term of office, on the jury service model.

These differing forms of stakeholder governance and combinations of direct and indirect democratic input should develop organically – this is a classic case of what matters is what works, and what works will depend on the size of the organisation, whether it serves a rural or urban population, and the enthusiasms and energies of the individuals who come forward. Government should establish the framework, and let a thousand flowers bloom.

Challenges and dilemmas

Inevitably, any government of the left interested in pursuing this agenda will face many issues and problems. The first challenge will be the classic tension between models of 'tight' and 'loose' management. For example, it is hard for any Labour Secretary of State to inherit huge power and influence over the running of the NHS, schools, social services, or any other area of the public services, and then simply give power away to others. The desire to use the centralised tools available to set national standards and to improve public services is enormously powerful. That after all has always been Labour's way.

There must be systems to ensure that basic minimum standards of service are guaranteed to all citizens. These can be regulated through national agreements, rigorous government systems of inspection and regulation, local service agreements and suppliers' contracts. But equality of standards need not mean sameness of delivery.

Local services can develop their own qualities and priorities, rooted in demographic and cultural differences. Local decision-making will mean differences in methods of service delivery and outcomes. Labour's devolution to Scotland and Wales has meant different approaches to social services, education, transport and other services. The powerful logic of decentralisation is that as more power and influence is devolved, greater differences in public services appear. Unlike the current situation, where the starkest differences in public services occur between deprived and affluent localities, under community control the differences will be between equally good, but different, public services.

There is nothing to fear from such a development. It will allow experimentation and innovation, which is a driver for improved quality. It will mean that certain areas will become celebrated for the excellence of particular services, within national service level guarantees.

What if innovation leads to failure? Here we need to distinguish between the failure of institutions and the failure of service delivery. Institutions and their senior management teams can be allowed to fail in pursuit of innovative solutions; we want risk-takers to drive forward improvement. But government must not allow innovation to be detrimental to service delivery, which is why government must be prepared to intervene to protect local services, as a last resort. If institutions and managers fail, government must tackle the failure head-on and be prepared to make radical changes to senior teams, and not allow secrecy or buck-passing.

A second dilemma will be the relationship between central funding and local expenditure. As more power passes to local communities, so funding must follow. Greater autonomy will be granted over budgets and investments, within a national framework. Community organisations which are granted powers to deliver public services will be subject to the same scrutiny and accountability as other public bodies, because they are responsible for public money.

What does this agenda mean for existing structures of local government? I see the development of community control as a way of enhancing and democratising local councils. It will challenge the traditional ways of doing business, but it will lead to a richer, deeper, more pluralistic local democracy.

More local partnerships between community groups, the council, social companies, and new networks and innovative forms of organisation will have to be created to deliver local services. These will operate in partnership and in parallel with local councils and other statutory bodies.

The role of councillors and councils will change. New elected bodies will challenge the traditional model of a group of two or three councillors representing a ward, and being responsible to local people for all of the local services. Instead, different elected representatives may be responsible for different services. Already in some areas with housing stock transfers, or new deal for communities schemes, a new diverse local democracy is developing where local people obtain a democratic mandate to run local services, but are not councillors. The way to tackle declining legitimacy and engagement in local politics is more, not less, local democracy.

Influence, control and choice

One of the aims – and results – of putting communities in control of local public services will be to increase the user-friendliness of the service they provide – and therefore the choices open to those they serve. Ownership of a public service means more than physical ownership of bricks and mortar; it means a practical sense of belonging, engagement and rights within the service. The exercise of influence within a public service is a key component of what a citizen should expect. One-size-fits-all public services are no longer appropriate or acceptable, whether it is in social services, education, health or housing. Today we expect more.

The freedom to choose is entirely dependent on your economic and social status. The poorer you are, the fewer choices you face in life. This is true of the obvious examples of choosing what holidays, cars, clothes and food to purchase, but more insidiously it is true of poorer people's choices within the public services. This recognition makes a mockery of the Conservatives' claims to be in favour of choice: what they mean is the freedom to choose for those that can afford it.

21

In deprived neighbourhoods, choice for local people has for long been diminished because public services, far from being universal and equal, have often been of poorer quality than those in prosperous areas. Now a plethora of area-based initiatives and schemes, including New Deal for Communities, Sure Start, neighbourhood and street wardens and so on, are in place now aiming to lift the quality of life and standard of public services for the very poorest citizens. By providing quality services, choice is being extended, thus allowing greater individual freedom and opportunities.

For choice in the public realm to be a reality for all, three parts of the system must work in concert:

- The individual citizen must have access to the channels of communication for articulating their choices to the provider
- There must be greater clients' influence and control over the means of allocating and using resources and systems for understanding benefits, risks and alternatives.
- The system must be flexible and responsive enough to be able to react to the demands of clients, to provide information to allow choice, and avoid value-judgements about the client and their wishes.

For choice to work, in other words, there needs to be community control over services. Citizens need to be empowered with understanding and knowledge of the system and the services, and have the confidence to articulate their views. This may depend on training, personal development and advocacy work. It means removing the barriers to access for lay people. It also means challenging the vested interests within the public services and tackling the 'we know what's good for you' syndrome.

Community ownership in public services

Community ownership offers a model of reform in many areas of public service. In housing, Labour councils in the past twenty years have effectively created a revolution in the patterns of ownership of social housing. The development of housing associations, housing co-operatives, and latterly the transfer of municipal housing to tenants' ownership and arms-length management organisations (ALMOs) has transformed the relationship between the resident and the housing provider. As the traditional relationship between the tenant and the council, based on an old style of municipal provision, was outpaced by tenants' demands for more control and ownership, more power has increasingly is being been passed to residents. The lessons we have learned are that small is beautiful, that local housing associations must be responsive to residents' needs and changing demands, and that the best way to get the service right is to involve residents in the development, prioritisation and delivery of the service itself. I believe that these objectives can often best be met through a major extension of locally controlled housing, and new forms of ownership and control by tenants. This might be an extension of the co-operative ideal, more stock transfers and arms length arrangements, democratic housing associations run by local people, or social companies raising money from the private sector.

In transport, an established example of a mutual oranisation is Ealing Community Transport, established as a co-op in 1979 by the local council. Today it comprises four companies, has 200 staff, and provides community transport and re-cycling to eight local authorities. A similar example is Greenwich Leisure, which was turned from a council department into a social enterprise, and in six years has trebled its income and halved its costs to the council. Its 1000 staff have a direct say in governance, planning and prioritisation.

The mutual idea works particularly well where high levels of trust are expected – for example in nursing and residential care or childcare. Here service users want to know that the main motivation for the service is quality of care, not financial gain. It could also work well where there is a deep reservoir of public goodwill and support, for example in local hospices.

But perhaps the largest opportunity for mutualisation of public services lies in the National Health Service. The NHS is a great success story and it is a living monument to socialism. It stands as proof that services delivered in the public realm can work, be popular, and be more efficient and cost-effective than private solutions. But it is also a creature of the times it was created. It is testament to the durability and popularity of the NHS that its basic structure and ethos survived, just, the onslaught of Thatcherism. But that survival has bequeathed to our Labour Government an organisation largely unchanged since in the 1940s.

If our society had not changed since Aneurin Bevan's time as health secretary, then there would be no great problem. But of course our society has transformed since the creation of the health service: seismic advances in technology and treatment, a revolution in patients' aspirations and demands, changes in work, family and culture, and a marked increase in life expectancy. These changes represent both a challenge and an opportunity for the NHS: a challenge to reform to meet new pressures and demands, and an opportunity to recreate an NHS true to its founding principles, but which extends and entrenches the principles of democracy and public and patient involvement in new ways.

The NHS is beginning to change from a top-down monolith, centrally controlled from Whitehall, and starting to take the first steps towards devolution of power and a wider range of providers. We are witnessing the development of a not-for-private-profit sector providing services within the NHS, and encouraging local people to have ownership over decisions about their health. This sector is most clearly seen at work in new primary care centres, homecare and residential care, and healthy living initiatives. There must be credibility and trust between the service deliverer, the provider, and broader local community. The governance of these services is often made up of local people who are keen to put something into the community, including any financial surpluses from their services. This reinvestment is particularly important for local people who are rightly sceptical and hostile to privatisation of the health service, and the replacement of the public good with private profit as the primary goal.

In my own community in Salford, local residents involved in the Government's New Deal for Communities initiative have designed two new health centres. One is aimed primarily at older people with a range of services including chiropody, complementary therapies, and chronic disease care, and the other is aimed at young families with a child clinic and links with the Sure Start initiative. Money has been made available through a public-private partnership to improve primary care buildings and facilities and through revenue support from the primary care trust (PCT). The centres will be run by local people who will employ the health workers themselves and services will be shaped by users and their families.

By moving away from services done to people, and towards services delivered with people, we improve the services themselves. There is strong evidence that public health is improved if people feel engaged with their treatment and take ownership over their own healthy living and well-being. A high level of public engagement in the health service is also a great way to deliver savings. The recent Wanless Report estimated that increased understanding, knowledge, self-help and engagement in public health by the public over the next twenty years could save the NHS £30 billion every year by 2022. That represents nearly half of the current NHS budget.

This is the principle behind the Government's drive for the creation of NHS foundation hospitals. There is a healthy debate being conducted about them. This is a useful starting point for the wider debate about public services I want to promote, and which this pamphlet is designed to inform. NHS foundation hospitals will be independent, not-for-profit institutions, run by staff, patients and the public with operational freedom and community ownership through a stakeholder board. They represent a new expression of public ownership. They will no longer represent a remote centrally administered machine directed from a distance by those at the top of the state, but genuinely local players sensitive to local needs delivering within a framework of essential national standards.

NHS foundation hospitals and trusts are the start, not the end of the process. We are merely dipping our toe in the water. Once the principle is established and the benefits are clear, I believe we should consider the extension of this mutual model to primary care trusts and other parts of the NHS, so as to create a network of not-for-profit providers operating within our national health service.

In health, and in other areas, this approach requires a new conceptual framework for considering public services. The new public services paradigm challenges the old idea of a centralised, bureaucratic, producer-led and elitist public sector. Instead we need to think of public services as locally-run, open, flexible and innovative.

If we are honest we must acknowledge that up to now 'public' ownership of health services, education, transport and other public services has been and remains for most working class people in Britain a chimera. Labour's task now is to make it a reality. This is a bold agenda, which threatens to challenge many cosy arrangements and assumptions, inside and outside the Labour Party. It also creates risk, and accepts that some decisions will be wrong and some experiments will fail. But the prize is the egalitarian society, cohesive community and individual liberty that socialists have always sought.

"

4 | Creating active citizenship

Central to the concept of communities in control is the idea of active citizenship. In Britain notions of citizenship are in many ways not as advanced or as important as in other democratic states. This may be because of our country's historical attachment to undemocratic institutions such as the House of Lords, or because of a rigid and ubiquitous class structure and the deference it bred. Without a written constitution or bill of rights, British citizens do not enjoy the same clear and codified menu of citizenship that others have. We have no pledge of allegiance in schools and feel uneasy about ostentatious displays of patriotism. That means that British citizenship is at best a passive state, at worst so vague as to lose meaning.

The development of citizenship as part of the schools' curriculum is welcome and overdue, but remains underdeveloped. Citizenship is about more than a reformed constitution and devolved state. Because power exists beyond the boundaries of politics, so citizenship needs to be exercised beyond the ballot box. We need to reform not just the structures of citizenship, but the culture of citizenship.

TH Marshall famously depicted citizenship in Britain as an historical progression from civil rights, to political rights, to social and economic rights. He rightly argued that citizenship was the antithesis of a class structure. It is precisely the development of citizenship in the social and economic spheres which concerns us here.

For citizenship to be meaningful it must be a daily activity, exercised with diligence and knowledge, not simply a guarantee of freedom from arbitrary state power and the right to vote once in a while. Citizenship must be an active not a passive condition. And because the dispersal of power in society is multi-faceted, so citizenship must be many-sided and pluralistic. That means that a democratic view of citizenship must include more than voting in elections, but also the right to be informed, engaged, and involved in a range of state activities and functions and a right to a meaningful stake in the public realm.

With these new rights come responsibilities. The corollary of the development of an enhanced sense of citizenship is an increased sense of mutuality, civic concern, and neighbourliness. By becoming aware of our own rights, we become more conscious of the rights of others. Citizenship can create a virtuous circle.

This socialist view of citizenship, as an active not passive state, should drive our reforms of public institutions and public services.

The citizens' participation agency

But there remains a practical problem. To populate the new structures of public involvement and ownership with effective citizens, we need to find and empower people to take on the role.

In the NHS, the new Commission for Patient and Public Involvement in Health (CPPIH) is designed to involve local people in local health services through the new patients' forums, which replace the community health councils (CHCs). Patients' forums will be made up of local people, and their main role is to provide input from patients on how local NHS services are run and could be improved. The CPPIH provides advice and training material to patients' forums and set standards for them, ensures that local people can have a say in decisions made about their health service, and reports to the Government on how the system of patient and public involvement in the NHS is working. I am attracted to the idea, advocated by the New Economics Foundation amongst others, of a national standard of governance and participation in the NHS. This would allow new models of governance to develop, whilst guaranteeing quality standards across the NHS.

Our experience in the NHS is a useful start, but we need to extrapolate this experience and apply it across the board. I believe we need a new national organisation to do this: a Citizens' Participation Agency. The Citizens' Participation Agency (CPA) would be a national body with a neighbourhood presence designed to encourage and support greater public involvement in every aspect of the running of the state: health, education, criminal justice, economic development, arts and leisure and so on.

We need to develop the capacity of the community to take control and ownership over decisions and services. Anyone involved in running a voluntary organisation, local group, or even a local party branch knows how hard it is to motivate people into action, and to persuade people to take on important but possibly dull responsibilities. I believe that local people will get involved over these decisions if they can genuinely answer for themselves the question 'what's in it for me?' The lesson from the early months of the New Deal for Communities scheme is that if people feel their efforts will be rewarded with tangible improvements to their local area and quality of life, they will volunteer their time, energy and effort. If change comes slowly, or not at all, people will soon become dispirited and drop out.

The CPA would equip citizens with basic democratic skills,

and give them the knowledge of how to work effectively inside the system, and how to challenge and change it. These skills have traditionally been taught inside political parties, trade unions, churches, voluntary groups, co-ops, temperance societies, women's groups, social clubs, adult education bodies, and other forms of self-organisation, but as these organisations have reduced in size and importance, these skills have been lost. It would encourage people to become Justices of the Peace, school governors, local councillors, NDC board members, regional development agency board members, prison visitors, arts board members, NHS trust members, housing association board members, and so on. It would run local courses and open days. It could issue accreditation and qualifications. It would serve to demystify the workings of local and regional services, and to break up the cosy cartels of the 'great and the good'.

The Citizens' Participation Agency would seek out and 'head-hunt' potential local leaders, giving confidence to people to learn more. It would be part Citizens' Advice Bureau, part Open University, part School for Social Entrepreneurs and part local recruitment consultants, fulfilling an active role in liberating people's potential and creating a new citizenship ethos at the local level.

Across government, in the Active Communities Unit in the Home Office, in the Neighbourhood Renewal Unit in the Office of the Deputy Prime Minister (ODPM), in the patients' participation work of the Department for Health and in the schools citizenship activity directed by the Department for Education and Skills (DfES), there is a significant amount of public money being spent on the promotion of active citizenship. But the effort is diffuse and lacks co-ordination. I believe we need to co-ordinate and consolidate this work, shift its emphasis, and create a new body which can capture the popular imagination and create a new culture of citizens' participation.

The structure of the CPA

I am not suggesting a new branch of central Whitehall administration designed to coerce us into becoming active citizens! The centralised top-down approach would not work. Once central government has established the principle and made central resources available, I favour the organic and devolved approach to organisation, letting different forms and styles emerge, dependent on local needs and cultures. Here, the impetus is for community activists and social entrepreneurs to come forward and decide locally how the Citizens' Participation Agency should perform in each locality.

One model might be to put the running of local CPA activity out to tender to not-for-profit organisations, so that the process of establishing the CPA serves as a catalyst to greater participation in itself. Another might be the form of organisation now being tried by local strategic partnerships (LSPs), which create strategic alliances between different parts of the local public, private and voluntary sectors.

We can learn from the high street presence of Citizens' Advice Bureaux, but also recognise the growing value of distance learning and teleworking. The new CPA can take the best of existing organisations and emulate it, and create new best practice of its own. What matters is that the structure of the CPA is designed around trust in local people and organisations, that central government should not interfere, and it addresses the needs of real, not imagined communities.

The functions of the CPA

What will the Citizens' Participation Agency do? The CPA's style of working should be entrepreneurial, flexible, risk-taking, and willing to cause trouble. Without wishing to be prescriptive, or attempting to create a blueprint, we can identify some of the key functions it should address:

Recruitment

At present, most active citizens form a self-selecting group. Usually this means the people who have had educational advantages, who are most articulate and organised, and who have the most resources. The first job of the CPA should be to search out potential community leaders and recruit them into learning, self-motivation, and taking on community activity. The CPA can help to create new ladders to such activism by identifying new local leaders, motivating and mentoring people, and providing encouragement and support.

Training and learning

The process of retreat from traditional self-run organisations has also meant that much of the learning or 'capacity-building' has been eroded. Where once a local political party branch, church or social club would allow active members to learn the skills of citizenship, now these skills are lost to the community. These skills might include advocacy, public speaking, accounts and budgeting, committee skills, campaigning, chairing skills, computing, desk-top design and so on. Learning these skills should be made available in a variety of interesting and innovative ways to local people. Underpinning these skills are other forms of citizenship education – about the processes and functions of democracy, how various institutions work, how to navigate complex bureaucracies, and how to gain and exercise power.

Information and campaigning

Because the CPA must be a pro-active organisation, part of its function should be campaigning and raising awareness in a locality. This should go beyond the passive provision of fact sheets and websites, and extend into lively advertising and marketing campaigns designed to motivate, radicalise and galvanise local people.

Advocacy

The CPA should have an advocacy role, enabling people to seek redress from organisations, private and public, by giving them support and help. Currently this role is conducted by local councillors, MPs, MEPs or members of devolved assemblies, by the Citizens' Advice Bureaux, by patients' advice and liaison service (PALS) in the NHS, or though members' organisations such as trade unions. As any MP, councillor, or CAB worker will tell you, the demand for advocacy outstrips the capacity to deliver it. The CPA cannot and should not replace the existing network of support, but it could help to co-ordinate the current arrangements, and help local advocates do their job. It would also serve to help citizens help themselves by giving them advice, information and support, rather than relying on others.

A new national framework

For this local activity to have a lasting and sustainable impact, it must be supported by a new national framework. I believe we need new levels of support at government level, for greater co-ordination between departments and initiatives, and for serious amounts of money to be allocated over ten to twenty years. Other measures could also help, such as the creation of 'social capital banks' to provide competitive financing for community investments which meet clear social objectives; incentives such as tax breaks for the private sector to allow their staff to be active citizens; and individual incentives for citizens to be involved, such as student loan write-offs, tax credits, and pension and national insurance entitlements to take account of voluntary activity. We must look at ways to reward and not to penalise those in receipt of benefits who undertake voluntary community activity.

66

5| Reading the book – case studies

Aneurin Bevan famously asked 'why gaze into the crystal, when you can read the book?' In many parts of the UK, and in many other countries, new forms of ownership, participation and engagement are being pioneered in the delivery of public services. As an MP and Minister I have been fortunate enough to meet some of the remarkable social entre-preneurs who are the inspiration behind these schemes, and to see for myself what local communities in control can achieve.

These case studies give us insight and understanding of what is possible and practical. The overarching lesson from these stories is that what matters is what works; socialism should not be about doctrines and blueprints, but about values and the ways they can drive social action and change. What works in Chicago may not work in Cheltenham. But the common strand in these examples – communities in control of their services (and destinies) – is an idea which transcends national systems and political cultures.

Case Studies

Westside Health Authority, Chicago US

Westside Health Authority (WHA) is a not-for-profit corporation rooted in the mostly African-American neighbourhoods of Chicago's west side. Since 1988 it has developed into a coalition of 50 partners including churches, community groups, clinics, hospitals, social services agencies and residents. WHA's mission is to improve opportunities for local residents to improve the health and well being of their community. It sees health and well being as dependent on social and economic opportunities as well as health care, and so works to create jobs and training, to improve buildings and the local environment, and to create networks for improvement and support. In 1996, the WHA developed the Every Block a Village (EBV) concept which encourages residents to identify with, and feel control over, their immediate neighbourhood. In each of 68 'villages' there are 'citizen leaders' who serve as a catalyst and focal point for neighbourhood renewal.

The work of the WHA includes cultural events, economic development, projects on fitness, nutrition, medical screenings and other healthy lifestyle work, development of gardens, murals, public art, and anti-litter campaigns, training in web technology, crime prevention and youth work. The WHA has raised $10 million for a health centre, purchased a closed hospital and used the buildings for homes, training, and health care, placed over 290 young people in health careers by connecting local schools and hospitals, and helped to reduce violence by 20 per cent.

Community Health Action Partnership in Salford (CHAPS)

In Kersal and Charlestown, the New Deal for Communities area in Salford, a group of local residents, two of whom were school governors and one who was a leader of a tenants' group, have come together to form Community Health Action Partnership in Salford (CHAPS). CHAPS has for the last 18 months been planning and designing a range of new health facilities for the neighbourhood. Some of the group have been through the 'expert patients programme' which enables people with long term chronic conditions such as diabetes and arthritis to become partners in their own health care and to manage their symptoms and treatment.

The programme, which is being piloted in the NHS and which so far has involved 2000 people nationally, appears not only to empower people as patients but also to encourage and enable them to take an active part in their communities. The CHAPS group have worked with NHS professionals and have designed two primary care centres, one concentrating on the needs of older people with podiatry, pharmacy, counselling and complementary therapies and one aimed at younger families with well persons clinics and links to the Sure Start programme.

They have now obtained a commitment from the LIFT Company (which is the Public Private Partnership which will rebuild and refurbish primary care facilities) of £2m capital to build the centres and they have secured ongoing revenue funding from the New Deal and the PCT to enable them to employ the health improvement workers in the community. CHAPS hopes in the future to run the centres as a local social enterprise giving residents the chance to own and run the facilities in accordance with local priorities.

CHAPS has just become a company limited by guarantee and is ready to negotiate with the LIFT Company the terms on which the centres will be held in the future. This is a radically different way of organising primary care when traditionally the NHS would have built a clinic, placed NHS staff in it, and provided a predictable range of services. CHAPS has consulted local people with a range of innovative methods including participatory appraisal and community visioning, often using methods from developing countries rather than conventional questionnaires. They are determined to use the buying power of the NHS to encourage local employment and procurement so that they get the double dividend of improved health care and local jobs with the well-recognised effect that employment has on community cohesion and individual well being

In Salford there is also an emerging citizenship training programme run by Proud City which can help to underpin community action and a very effective School for Social Entrepreneurs which helps people to achieve their dreams of establishing viable social enterprises with community benefits. As the local chair of CHAPS, Helen Reed, observes: 'There is a solid community that still exists in this area, but somewhere along the line it has lost its voice. We are empowering residents to give them back their voice.'

Health Action Centres in Cheltenham

Cheltenham is not the most likely place to spring to mind when considering how to make health services more accessible to poor and excluded communities but alongside the undoubted affluence of some parts of the borough there is also poverty, deprivation and long term ill health particularly on some of the more isolated estates. In these areas nearly 8000 households have family members with a limiting long term illness, over 5000 residents have a work-limiting disability, half the area has the highest coronary heart disease and stroke mortality in under-65s in the South West, and a third of families are on income support.

Over the last five years neighbourhood projects have been

developed in eight communities pioneering initiatives to meet local health needs such as estate based user led, community managed mental health support services, support groups for a range of vulnerable residents and income maximisation for people with long term conditions. They have established eight health action centres on the estates with surgeries providing support with all aspects of residents' lives including drugs, debt, domestic violence counselling and youth advocacy. They are expanding to provide accessible bases for ante- and postnatal care, mobile dentists, coronary rehabilitation and family planning. They have strong links with the neighbourhood college encouraging healthy learning and learning for health through basic skills education.

The projects have been supported by the co-operative movement and have developed several community enterprises which are run by local people and are creating jobs and services in the neighbourhood. As Bernice Thomson, a resident of Hestersway put it: 'For years we have campaigned for adequate health services on the Hestersway estate. The opportunity to develop a new healthy living centre has been made possible because of strong partnership working between the community, the neighbourhood project, the PCT and other health partners.'

Newham Food Access Partnership

The Food Access Partnership was set up by residents of Newham in 2001 and has grown rapidly from one small project into a total of 16 community led food co-ops across the borough, breakfast clubs in local schools, luncheon clubs for older residents, a healthy food box scheme run in conjunction with Sure Start for young families, fruit tuck shops in schools and clubs, cook and eat schemes, a healthy café, a home delivery service, community growing projects and juice bars. Its aim is to promote and encourage healthy eating, to supply quality fresh fruit and vegetables to families on low incomes at affordable prices and to build the skills and knowledge of local people in buying and preparing fresh food.

It is clear now that eating more fruit and vegetables can lead to a reduction in cancer coronary heart disease and stroke by up to 20 per cent and it is also clear that the poorest people eat less fruit and vegetables than those who are better off. Without a car to get to the supermarket and without decent local shops it can cost 50 per cent more for poorer people to get hold of decent quality produce

The Newham project has brought together all those involved in local education and regeneration and has made a massive impact on the health and well being of local people. All of the co-ops are led and managed by local people which has helped to engender a much stronger sense of community involvement, it has increased social capital and given people the skills and confidence to become involved in a wide range of regeneration projects. The links with primary care have meant that those with long term conditions such as diabetes can have access on prescription to £3.50 worth of fruit and vegetables per week from the co-op. They are beginning to employ local people creating jobs and opportunities through community enterprise which will bring a double benefit to the area in employment and health improvement.

A local Newham resident explained the project simply: 'By working together in our food co-ops, breakfast clubs and cooking projects we have not just helped people eat more healthily but also built a stronger sense of community and begun to take control in many other areas of our lives.'

What lessons can we learn?

The central theme of this pamphlet is that working class people can, with support, training, information and encouragement, take control in their own communities and create public services which are much more responsive, accessible and valued by local people. As a councillor, MP and chair of a regeneration board in Salford I have seen for myself local residents gradually developing skills and confidence and starting to exercise a greater degree of power and decision making in how public services should be run and delivered. As Minister responsible for public involvement and now as Public Health Minister I have visited a wide range of organisations including the West Side Health Authority in Chicago to find out how poor communities are beginning to come together to share their skills and talents and develop new models of community ownership of health facilities, underpinned by citizen leadership, and driven by the desire to bring hope to communities excluded from the mainstream.

I have been struck by the similarities between the two communities in Salford and Chicago and yet they are operating in very different environments. In Salford the group is working to develop community health facilities under the umbrella of a fully tax funded NHS and is able to access public money to support its ideas. In Chicago the people involved have had to struggle to create their ideas despite a health system that provides little or no support to the poorest communities. My encounters with local people in Chicago made me think that if they could succeed despite the system and bring together their ideas and enterprise to create high quality health services for some of the poorest people then what could we achieve if we were able to liberate the same sense of energy imagination and enterprise in our communities backed up and positively encouraged by our health system which is now better resourced than ever before?

In Cheltenham the eight health action centres have been established through the drive and enthusiasm of local people and support from the highly successful Oxford Swindon and Gloucester Co-op Society and are only just beginning to tap in to the resources from the mainstream NHS via the Primary Care Trust. They provide a radical new model for primary care services that are community led and managed. Commissioners are beginning to appreciate that investing in local enterprises can be effective in terms of improved health outcomes, the creation of jobs for local people and very good value for money for the NHS.

In Newham the links between the food access co-ops, the regeneration partnership local schools and the Primary Care Trust are essential to maximising the impact of the investment made. Fresh fruit and vegetables are 40 per cent cheaper than in the supermarkets, they are available on prescription for people with long term conditions such as diabetes, the co-ops provide a lively social occasion, an opportunity for positive health promotion and are completely led and managed by local residents themselves. It is hard to think of a more effective way of tackling health inequalities and empowering local communities than through the food we eat.

All of these case studies are real evidence of the capacity and willingness of local people to become involved as active participants in improving their health facilities taking responsibility for their own health and well being and extending their own skills and knowledge. The challenge for government is to ensure that these projects are not just temporary examples of innovation but become part of the mainstream of the NHS and an essential component of the healthy communities we are trying to engender through all of our myriad regeneration programmes.

The key question is whether as politicians we really are brave enough to devolve power and resources not just to the frontline staff in our public services but to take the crucial extra step and devolve power and decision making to local people themselves.

6| Apathy or activism?

There is a myth in British politics that people are 'apathetic'. This myth, largely disseminated by the media, is based on voting figures for recent elections. It is not borne out by anyone who has knocked on a door wearing a rosette, leafleted in a shopping centre, or listened to a constituency surgery. The people that politicians and activists meet are rarely 'apathetic'. They are more often opinionated, passionate, angry, alienated, occasionally pleased, but rarely apathetic. Ask a voter about local parking, burglary, dog fouling, the state of local hospitals, roads or parks, the euro or Britain's asylum policy, and see how apathetic they sound. If newspaper leader writers are doubtful, I would invite them to spend a Saturday morning at Salford Precinct and hear for themselves.

It is true to say that recent election turn-outs for national, European and local elections have fallen dramatically. This should give us serious cause for concern, and new ways of encouraging voter registration turn-out and political engagement must be found. But voting cannot be seen as the sole indicator of political or civic engagement. As Pippa Norris points out in her book *Democratic Phoenix* there are many countervailing trends and forces in modern democracies which challenge the pessimists' views. She shows that across the world, new forms of protest, engagement and activism are attracting serious levels of support. She writes: 'the pervasive idea that the public has become disengaged from every form of civic life over-simplifies a far more complex and messy reality.'

The choice for democrats is to re-invent democratic systems to reflect changes in aspiration and expectation, and in technology. There are many well-rehearsed arguments about the ways democracy can be enhanced through postal ballots, changes to electoral systems, electronic voting, changing the opening times and locations of polling stations, and these are all worth exploring. Increased turnouts in postal ballots in the 2003 local elections are encouraging. For example, across my city Salford the average turnout in the postal ballot in the 2003 local elections was 40.7 per cent, compared to 25.07 per cent in a traditional poll in 2002. A similar pattern of markedly higher turnouts emerged in the 58 other local authority areas where postal ballots were used.

Structures and cultures

But reforms to the structure of democracy, whilst necessary and overdue, are not enough. We need to change the culture of democracy, with the democratisation of huge swathes of public life. This does not mean more elections for more public officials. The experience of the US shows that you can have layer upon layer of democratically-elected officials, from judges to dog-catchers, but it does not lead to a more democratic society. Democracy in much of America, like belonging to an exclusive country club, has become the pursuit of the established, wealthy and articulate minority. A culture of democracy is not deter-mined by how many votes you have to cast for others, but by what stake and say you have over decisions which affect you. It is about the daily exercise of your own personal citizenship in myriad ways.

In that context, I hope that my argument for community control over many more areas of the public realm can be seen as part of a broader and deeper democratisation of society, which will substantially assist in the revitalisation of politics in its widest sense.

There are already signs of hope. The lessons from the New Deal for Community board elections are that if people feel that their efforts will be rewarded, that their voices will be heard, and that they can make a difference in their own community, then they will come forward for election, and vote.

These community elections have been analysed in detail by Professors Rallings and Thrasher. They reveal several important features:

- A key motive for standing for election was 'to put something back'
- A key motivator for getting involved is dissatisfaction with local authority provision
- Voter disengagement results from a distrust of authority and a sense of powerlessness
- The higher the levels of neighbourhood deprivation, the lower the turnout
- Electors found alternative voting methods easy to understand
- In some areas voter turnout was significantly higher than for the council elections, especially where there is active campaigning, media attention, and involvement by local leaders
- All-postal voting is the most effective way of increasing turnout.

In Sheffield, Bradford, Bristol, Newcastle, Rochdale, Tower Hamlets, Newham and Walsall turnout for the NDC board elections was higher than for the council. In Bristol and Sheffield, turnout reached over 50 per cent – double the turnout for the council elections. These lessons must be well learned by all.

Most working class people do not have the time for endless committees and altruistic endeavour. It is the middle classes who tend to have the time for charity work and noble causes. Working people are too busy working, perhaps in more than one job, to devote their leisure time to activities beyond the home and family. So the rewards must be obvious and the results swift if single mums, piece-rate workers, shift workers, or multiple-jobbers are to be involved in community activity. I hope too that my proposal for a Citizens' Participation Agency would reach out to a new cadre of engaged citizens, to form the next generation of activists and leaders.

There are plenty of people on the right of politics who want to denude the public realm of its life and vitality, to debase public services, and to discredit the idea of collective provision. If public services work and are popular, it challenges and undermines their philosophy of the market being the best route to human happiness. The ideological battle between private and public is still being waged, but its terms have changed. Labour is expanding its armoury of public provision and deepening the scope of the public realm, whilst the Tories are distilling their solutions to raw, uncut privatisation of the public services, beyond even the boundaries of Thatcherism.

What seems clear is that if we do nothing to pass power to local communities, the result will not be apathy; it will be alienation and anger. Our choice is between giving people control over their lives, or failing to deliver the transformation we want. The great lesson from the successes and failures of social democracy in Britain and around the world is that social change cannot come simply by pulling the levers and pressing the buttons in central government departments, or by relying on an enlightened and altruistic political class. Social change must be a common endeavour of all citizens, if change is to be progressive and lasting. We need to breathe new life into our neglected neighbourhoods, we need to spread a message of hope that politics matters, and we need to put communities in control.

Wealth's Fair Measure
The reform of inheritance tax

Inheritance tax has become extremely unfair. It is paid by the moderately affluent – especially those in the Southeast where house prices have risen above the £250,000 tax threshold – but not by the very wealthy, who can largely choose to avoid it. In *Wealth's Fair Measure: The reform of inheritance tax*, Ruth Patrick and Michael Jacobs argue that reform is needed as the current rules of exempting gifts made more than seven years before death and providing reliefs for private businesses and agricultural land makes avoidance easy for the wealthy .

In the Foreword to the report, Bill Gates Sr, father of the billionaire Miscrosoft founder Bill Gates, lends his support to the Fabian proposals and links them to the growing campaign in the United States against President Bush's proposal to abolish US estate tax. The reform of inheritance tax is also analysed here by experts including representatives of HM Treasury and the Irish Revenue.

April 2003 ⁿ ISBN 0 7163 3057 1 ⁿ £9.95

Available from the Fabian Society bookshop 020 7227 4900 or email bookshop@fabian-society.org.uk